Songs of the Salt Pond

Songs of the Salt Pond

20 YEARS IN KEY WEST

Michael E. Hayes

PALMETTO
P U B L I S H I N G
Charleston, SC
www.PalmettoPublishing.com

Paperback: 979-8-8229-4002-4
eBook: 979-8-8229-4003-1

Dedication

This book is dedicated to my wife, Suellen,
whose spirit is responsible for it.
I greatly regret she is not here to read it.

Table of Contents

Introduction

The Salt Ponds in Key West once covered a hundred acres of man-made shallow pans carved into the coral of the island. Suspended during the Civil War and abandoned several times, the commercial salt-making operation ended by 1906.

This is a book of poems about life and Key West. The Salt Pond is my Koi Pond, and I have spent many hours looking out at it, thinking, and meditating.

An Autobiography of Loss

An Autobiography of Loss

Watching the pelicans glide above the breakers
I am not certain if life has been easy on me,
or,
have I been too kind to myself?
They cruise in a military formation.

When my grandparents died
I was still young and my life was not disrupted.
Spotting fish,
the pelicans plunge.

My mother died in 1992.
She was hospitalized in Sun City, Arizona.
For a week we visited her.
She spoke to my father,
ignored me.
On the flight back to Connecticut
I cruised at an angry speed.

Terns flew in formation just above the waves.
My father remarried,
adopted his new family,
dismissed his old.
The terns circled back for a second run.
You could see the fish boiling on the surface.
My father died in 2012 at ninety-five.
The last few years
he either did not know who I was,
or,

knowing,
demanded what did I want.
As the waves broke,
the bait was silvery and evident.
Birds flocked.

In 2018, my wife of forty-five years died.
Bigger fish drove the bait towards shore.
More birds came.
This was my first real loss.

Taken

The apartment is empty.
I am alone.
My partner of forty-five years is gone;
she was taken.
It is empty
except for the profound sadness
that awaits my daily return.
It is there without fail.
It is empty,
not of memories
but of life.

Many years ago,
much younger and less confident,
I asked my wife if she really loved me.
Her reply was *I haven't left yet, have I?*
It was a foolish question,
and she did not tolerate my foolishness.
She could have left at any time,
but never did.
She was taken.

Her last words,
a day before she was taken,
were *Get a life.*
I still work
and see friends,
I am learning not to tolerate foolishness,
and I struggle to get a life.

She Knew

At the time,
my mind was clouded by hope
and would not let me see otherwise.

She was dying,
she knew it,
but admitted it to no one.
The illusion of hope being fragile,
she took great care
to keep it from breaking.

But she knew,
her body knew,
and instead of using her strength
to live,
she used what was left
to protect the ones she loved.

She would have chosen to fly.
To soar on the thermals,
but honesty,
like gravity,
would not let her.
She was stuck to a ground
that was unforgiving.

She accepted it,
did not like it,
but remained focused,
and,
when no one was looking
in the early morning hours,
she left.

The Salt Pond

The Salt Pond

If you go beyond the Salt Pond's
serenity,
past the horseshoe crabs
crawling along its muddy bottom,
past the land crabs digging deeper
into their holes.

If you go west,
there is a circus
offering hopes, promises,
and good times.

Trapeze artists
fly untethered,
clowns are everywhere.
Spider-Man rides his bicycle,
Wonder Woman cakewalks down the street,
and young women
in tutus
wave to the gawking crowds.

She would have urged my participation—
to join with the magic,
to dance to the calliope—
but I have chosen not to.

It is the Salt Pond,
not the circus,
that holds our memories.

Windblown Memories

It is late in the afternoon
The sky above the Salt Pond is gray with rain.
The clouds come from the northeast
bringing darkness and memories.

In Taos,
the storm clouds rolled down from
the Sangre de Cristo Mountains.
They were heavy and hung in the valley.
The world became smaller,
more intimate.

We were there for a summer,
staying with my family.
Difficult,
but doable,
I miss our shared times.

You would not approve of me dwelling
on such things.
At the end, you told me
Get a life,
but you,
in so many, many ways,
were my life.

Not an Easy Promise

It's been raining off and on for several days.
The bottom of the Salt Pond is muddy.
The tide flows in slowly;
each day presents yet a different view.

Promises made from love are difficult to keep.
It is not the fear of breaking them,
but the fear of falling short
that haunts me.

I watch an osprey,
gliding by at eye level,
looking for food.
A great white heron stalks the pond.
The wind is honest
but carries mixed messages from beyond the reef.

Each day
I swim.
Sometimes in the rain.
I walk the high-water line of the ebbing tide;
I eat thoughtfully
and get good sleep.

I have promised my children
and my wife,
almost three years gone,
to take care of myself.

To live life
and not just wait.

I have found that such a commitment,
fashioned from years of love
and great respect,
is not an easy one to keep.

Three Birthdays Later

This is my third time around the sun
since you have died.
It has not gotten easier,
but it has become more tolerable.
My tears these days
are shed inwardly,
watering our memories.

I have not yet formed new memories,
and I remain unconnected.

There are times,
I fear,
that I have not kept my promise to you.
I wander,
loyal to the past,
not willing to embrace the future.

I keep to myself
and I write.
My poems seek connections,
and they are the vessels for my grief.

Karmic Wound

I have come to believe
that there has been a hole in my soul
from the very, very beginning.
It has taken many shapes.
Circles, rectangles, squares,
and shapes not yet able to be named.
But for sure,
there is a hole,
and for sure,
it has always been there.

My family used words,
many words,
but did few deeds.
I have learned not to trust words.
They do not have the timeless truth
of the phases of the moon
or the rhythm of the tides.

So,
like a blind person
whose touch defines his reality,
yours defined mine,
and its loss—
that is the shape of the hole.

Like Ferlinghetti, I Am Waiting

I no longer have memories.
I am visited instead by ghosts of the past.
Cued by some unknown force,
they slip in from the *llaño quemado* as
dry and fragile as
windblown sagebrush.

Sometimes they pass so quickly
that I am in doubt of their existence.
It is difficult to believe that these things have happened,
but the pain and joy I feel
tell me they are true.

Had I not grown to know you as I did,
I would have missed a wonder.
I would have never known
that magic can be real.

The Old Ones
who speak of magic in my dreams
call softly across the *llaño*
in the winds of night.
Their spirits are restless.

I too am restless.
I think about you always,
waiting,

waiting,
continuously waiting.
Waiting
for a rebirth of wonder.

Key West Cold

Thursday night at the Green Parrot,
I am standing alone in the crowd.
Mostly locals,
mostly with AARP cards.
The floor is packed,
the band and dancers have merged.

Outside it is cold for Key West.
There is no ice on the Salt Pond,
no children playing pickup hockey,
but it is cold outside.

Not Icelandic cold.
Not bone-chilling cold.
Not the wind-piercing cold
that makes you yearn for hot soup
and woolen socks,
but cold enough for jeans and hoodies.
Cold enough to abandon
flip-flops and shorts.

I observe the dancers as they feel the music;
I envy the warmth of couples.
I am standing with my back to the wall
watching,
and I am cold.

Iceland: A New Day

Across the Florida Straits
a cloud bank holds solid,
forming an impenetrable curtain.
It has restrained me
as only clouds can do.

For four years
I have been struggling
against the bonds of sadness,
never sure
if I wanted to break them.

Today is different.
I am bold,
I am eager,
and I am nervous as
I step out the door.

I am off on an adventure
of wishful magnitude.
I am taking my sadness with me,
but it is the willingness to be excited
that propels my feet.

Iceland: South Coast

Iceland: Ode to My Muse

I walked a tide line of volcanic wants.
A black sand beach where winds
of change challenged my equilibrium
and lava flow carved the shoreline.

Yet,
I dream of gentler shores,
calm waters,
and silent rainbows.
The rhythm of the Salt Pond
sets my day.

But you,
you have always been beyond my reach
As unpredictable and elusive
as the Northern Lights.

You,
you have been eruptive to my serenity.
You pull me from the quiet of the Salt Pond's
rhythm.
And yet,
even though you are beyond my fervent wishes,
you center me.

The South Coast of Iceland

Iceland: Coming Home

The Salt Pond stretches out before me.
In the shallow waters,
egrets search for food.
The tide is coming in,
and there is a slight breeze from the east.

Here,
I am at home.
The Salt Pond holds me.
It is where I live.
Leaving it
is always emotional
and seemingly a risk.

We were companions for almost two weeks.
A long time for people living alone.
We saw volcanoes, waterfalls, lava fields,
and glaciers.
A beautiful
but
unfriendly landscape,
so unlike the Salt Pond.

We were unsure how we would do together—
sharing personal space is not our thing.
At the end of our northern adventure,
we still were friends.
Strong friends,
sharing truths.

The egrets are roosting now,
a cluster of white dots across the water.
Rain must be on the way.

To have you so close but so far away
was difficult.
I am happy to be home,
but
I am missing the closeness of your distance.

Salt Pond Sunrise

Ode to a Lady on a Couch

At a time when I could stare at the ocean
without wonder,
when my heart felt only emptiness and
sadness,
when the days went by with fragile hope,

you,
you gave me
transcendental medication.

Little Things

Losing you assaulted me like a tsunami.
A wild incoming tide.
One without warning,
an ambush
flooding my reason.

So now,
as the waters recede,
there is a calmness
that comes.

We will no longer debate
how hot or cool to keep the house.
How the dishwasher should
or should not be loaded.
Or
whether the toilet paper should unroll from the top
or from the bottom.

I miss the passion of these debates,
conversations that were so intense
but really
did not matter.

Me Too

Last evening,
as I listened to Billy Collins read
"Me First",
I thought of you.
I am still in awe that you
picked me.

From the very beginning,
you were so certain about us.
It took me a while longer,
but I too
came to that same conclusion.

Many years later,
children grown and gone,
still together,
living in Key West,
you mentioned to a friend
with that same absolute certainty
that you thought I would precede you
in death.

As if
by saying it
it was an indisputable fact,
a certainty.

However,
you miscalculated
and
I sit here,
sipping my morning coffee.

Early Christmas Morning

It's early Christmas morning,
and I sip my coffee as it cools.
Years ago,
in New Hampshire,
we left sooty footprints on the hearth,
to our children's delight.

Today,
the salt pond stretches before me.
Roosting birds have left,
and the house,
like the Salt Pond,
is empty.

In Taos,
Christmas was communal.
Friends and strangers gathered
on the hard-packed ground of
the ancient pueblo,
between the kivas,
waiting,
waiting for Vespers to end.

Waiting to join the Virgin's procession
as she blessed
the six cardinal points
of the Tewa world.

This morning,
sitting alone,
the past floats by.
Christmas clouds,
New Hampshire, Taos, Connecticut,
now Key West.
On this early
Christmas morning,
I am opening only good memories.

Taos Pueblo

One Family

Key West

It was a chilly day at the circus.
The gossamer wings on the angel
were as cold as the drink in his hand.
He rode an old bicycle
and wore bright white briefs with a tutu
it was still early evening.
His wings quivered in the wind

The bunny was at the Green Parrot,
Fully costumed
and the lights had yet to dim.

Men and women,
would-be aerialists,
were already balancing high on their wire.

Ink everywhere,
painted bodies,
colored memories,
all part of the daily parade.

Spectators from normal lives,
stunned,
but unaware that,
if they stayed too long,
they too
would become performers
beneath the tropical big top.

I sit and watch,
long ago having been assigned
to the chorus of clowns.

There is a loneliness
to the circus's intimacy,
a tropical sadness
lurking underneath the big top.

Key West

Wet Foot, Dry Foot

Hers was not the face
that launched a thousand ships.
If there was beauty,
it was in the furrows of her pain.
She had looked at life with broken hope
but was ready to risk what little left she had.

The voyage had been tough;
the chug leaked,
the Chevy engine failed,
and they had drifted for several days beneath
an unforgiving sun.

Two people died, water ran out,
no food remained.
The ocean had had its way.
Progress seemed an illusion,
a mirage.

And when land came,
it called to her.
She waded through the shallow water
to the beach,
joyful at having warm sand between her toes,
and then,
like so many others before her,
She disappeared into the night.

Cuban Chug

Freaks Grown Old

They were never called dive bars back then,
just shady places frequented by men in jeans,
army fatigues
long hair,
ponytails,
and beards.

Proud women with long hair,
beads,
big earrings.

Talk was of Vietnam and politics,
drugs and music.
Cheap beer flowed.

Proud children of the Dharma Bums,
of the Hog Farm,
proud children of the road.
All old now.

It is Thursday night at the Green Parrot,
Key West.
The jukebox is playing something old.
Sometimes Janis is heard.
The band is on break.

Men,
veterans of internal wars,
beer in hand,
hair still long,
ponytails now gray,
old ink,
nodding to familiar rhythms.

Women too,
hair gray,
some with streaks of red and blue,
earrings,
beads.
They dance
as if time has not passed.

Fifty years later,
freaks still proud
and still doing their thing.

The Green Parrot

Song of the Turtle Lady

She was the turtle lady;
she had been married many times,
single now,
never had children,
but she cared for turtles.

From March to October
she walked the beach,
looking for signs of nesting.
She guarded the eggs
and spoke to them.
She told them tales of tides,
of cross currents,
of predators.
She had become their protector;
they had become her purpose.

She counted the nests
and could tell you
how many eggs had
successfully hatched.

Once back in the water,
however,
the turtles were on their own,
and she hoped she had taught them well.

She spoke of them as family,
invited them back,
but. like her always present bottle of wine,
the nests,
eventually, were empty.

Not Her Home

The dogs were playing behind the shed,
sniffing at the newly cut wood.
Snow was in the air;
snow was already on the ground.
Good weather soon would turn bad.

The dogs circled the newly stacked wood
and turned toward the house.
The wind carried the smoke of a wood stove.

She did not like the cold
nor the coming snow.
She was of a summer clime:
shorts, tank tops, and flip-flops.

Why she lived up north was a long story
involving love, loyalty, and children,
but it was not her heart's home.
She longed for the comfort
of warm sand beneath bare feet.

The dogs,
excited
by the coming change,
chased scents made sharper by the cold.

She, though,
was not excited.

No longer was this a novelty,
just snow
and a time for boots.

Snow Sky

Again

Always struggling to stay aloft,
he wished to be as free as the skimmers
flying low over the waves,
but cross winds,
cross currents,
carried him to other places.

The winds blew him to the edge of his world,
to the very rim.
A place of peril
ruled by
evil riptides and demon moons.

He had been there before.
He was there now,
but this time he stopped,
letting go the possibility
of an infinite chemical night.

Queen of the Nile

She was already there,
waiting with imperial arrogance.
She sat erect
with expectation that everything would
revolve around her in a Ptolemaic orbit.
I was a moon to her sun.

She came with ambiguous problems,
issues dramatically presented
but never quite defined.
Each was fueled by an impatience
with a need to be solved immediately.

And when they weren't,
her anger was a solar storm.
With illogical sun spots creating therapeutic
static and disrupting communication.

She was Nefertiti, Consort of the Sun,
The Great Royal Wife of Akhenaten,
Queen of the Nile,
and she made sure you knew it.

She leaned far forward,
showing an ample amount of herself.
Do you like me?
to which
there was no safe answer.

Waiting for the Big Bang

He was manic and scattered.
The words tumbled from his mouth
like marbles from a bag.

He knew the answers,
he knew the questions,
he knew it all.

Like a shooting star
in a collapsed universe,
he shot across the sky
with a certainty
that only he could have.

His exploits were cosmic,
universal,
galactic.
There were no red dwarfs,
no black holes.

He thought he had total control.
And we,
we just sat there
waiting for the big bang.

Sunrise over the Salt Pond

Love of Sunrise

The morning sky was reflected on the ocean's swells.
It was glass-like.
A white heron waded in a tidal pool.
The sun was not yet warm.
He loved the mornings.
They were silent and the noises of the day
had not yet begun.

But for her,
the mornings were very different.
They began somewhere long ago
in the middle of an oceanic night.
She could not say when,
but it seemed to have been always.

She was not fond of sunrises,
not fond of mornings.
That is when her body came alive,
when the creatures began to move.

She could feel them in her bones.
She could smell them;
they had the odor of rubbing alcohol,
and they whispered things.

They resisted extermination, medications, prayers,
diets, love, and
wishful thinking.
It made no difference,
each morning they would start again.

So sunrise was not her favorite time.
Sleep was her protector,
a blanket of respite.

She did not love sunrise,
certainly not the way he did.

Struggling to Stay Afloat

Even as a child,
he knew he was different.
He heard voices and saw things that others didn't.

As he grew,
so did the things of which he
learned not to speak of.
At times they were vivid and
he reacted to them violently,
talked to them harshly.

At nineteen,
they became religious;
they dictated rituals.
He was at sea without a rudder,
the real and the unreal
merged into a hypnagogic storm.

Life was a whirlpool,
and he struggled to stay afloat.
There were days of confusion,
days of drugs,
days of vodka,
days without medication.

The ocean raged in his head.
There were squalls without respite,
but there were also a few days
when the wind lay down
and the sun
reflected off the surface
of calmer thoughts.

None of this was predictable,
and it drew him further and further
from solid land.

Hypnagogic Storm

From beyond the airport
and the mangroves,
from beyond the waters of the Salt Pond,
an unnamed storm
flooded her shoreline.
It left flotsam, jetsam, and terror.
It left questions
without answers.
It left many,
many unknowns.

The damage was hidden
far beneath the surface.
She knew,
but she didn't know.
She had buried it on the bottom,
beyond the coral reef,
in the deepest of deep waters.

It stayed there,
almost completely covered,
until,
when the moon
did not guard her sleep closely,
it surfaced as lagan.
Rising from the deep,
it barely breached the surface,
but terror,
terror was still its companion.

Depression*

I sit quietly at my desk;
the Black Dog is off to my left.
Today I have the patience of Penelope.
The only movement is my internal tide.

Today
I am calm
as is the dog.

There have been growls,
snarls, canine threats,
but today the dog is quiet,
placid.

Life has changed,
and the space that had been filled
with warmth and flowers
now belongs to the dog.
It lies there patiently,
waiting,
a steel trap.

I try to keep it at bay,
sometimes successfully,
sometimes not.
It follows me everywhere,
everywhere I go,
with a fierce loyalty
I value not.

*Hemingway, Churchill and others referred to depression as
"The Black Dog."

Hemingway's Dog by Sean P. Callahan

Hamartia

The boat glided easily through the gulf waters;
dolphins played in the bow's wake.
There were pelicans, gulls,
and frigate birds above.

The salt air was exhilarating.
Hand in hand they stood,
leaning against each other for support,
as always.
They were laughing in awe
at the sea,
the sky,
the dolphins.
It was a bright blue day.
Small islands and fishing shacks dotted the channel.

The euphoria was the togetherness,
not the ride.
He turned to her and said
Let's get remarried.
She quickly replied *We can't,*
I'm dead.

There Was No Balm in Gilead

Each time he left it was with the firm belief,
fashioned by the demons of his detoxes,
that this time,
he assured me,
would be the last time.

The Fates, however, were not on his side.
They played with him,
allowing only short-term successes,
like a skyrocket exploding in the night
and then crashing to the sea.
His life was the steel ball working its way
through the maze,
careening off the sides
and then falling into a hole,
short of its goal.

At an early age, he dreamed of being someone,
having a family.
He had even named his first child,
Benjamin,
the second would be Ellen,
but his course went awry.

His father was more comfortable with his older brother.
There was a ten-year difference,
and they were ten thousand emotions apart.
It hurt,

it stung,
all the way to his inner,
tender self.

He needed balm,
but there was no balm in Gilead,
so he drank,
and he drank
and he drank.

He had been to rehabs in California,
Ohio, Florida, and other places.
They all told him the same thing:
stop drinking.
But he didn't,
he couldn't,
he wouldn't.
The wound was too deep and it never healed.

He lost jobs, girlfriends, places to live, self-respect,
and finally his dignity.
What else was there left to lose,
so he drank.

He sat there opposite me now ready to leave,
sober and clean.
I wished him good fortune,
he told me he was through, it was the end,
no more.

He was going to stop.
I hoped so.
I believed he believed,
but what really had changed?

Seaweed

She was old, very old,
like the constant rhythm of the tides.
She was moon-wise
to a depth greater than the ocean's deep.
She was as sharp as the salt air
on a cold winter's morning.
She had sea glass style,
old and smooth,
but her family did not see it.

Her family no longer needed her and
she was jetsam to be thrown overboard.
Did it really matter if she sometimes got the day wrong,
the date wrong?

Her family,
using love as a disguise,
saw only what they wanted,
and they abandoned her to the drift.

White Rabbits

It is the first of yet another month.
Walking along the beach,
the tide,
after banging against the seawall all night,
is placid.

Early morning fog makes the shrimp boats
seem like whooping cranes
hovering above the water.
Their nets
extend like wings,
ready for flight.

I, too, am ready to fly,
to spread my wings
and soar,
but to where?

My thoughts hover in the morning mist.
There is magic to this time of day.
I can feel it in the sand beneath my toes.
It is in the dampness of the salt air.

Quietly,
I whisper an incantation of good fortune.
Magical words,
learned a long, long time ago.

The fog,
clinging closely to the ocean's surface,
muffles the invocation.
The shrimp boats, like dragonflies,
hover.

Sunday Morning

It is Sunday morning,
a New York Times morning,
and I am feeling completely calm.
The tide is high
and the Salt Pond full.

My mind is quiet,
at rest,
demons sleep.
Something,
something yet to be acknowledged,
seems to have been put to rest.

Winged memories
are not flying into stubborn winds.
They are roosting
like the birds last night.
The world is still.

It is Sunday morning
and I am waiting,
waiting for Noah
and his magic boat.

Tango in Key West

We sat in the corner of the studio;
we talked about his paintings,
my poems, the week's events,
but mostly about how we are haunted by creativity.

The act of creation is a mystery,
a dance of bubbles,
each with its own rhythm and depth.
Poems and paintings
come up from the dark.
Bubbles that pop to the surface
and take form,
with a hurricane of mental energy.

And as it passes,
when it is done,
there is an emptiness
which is frightening.

We talked often about this experience,
sitting against the back wall
in the corner,
drinking coffee.
Neither of us,
no matter how deeply we have looked,
can understand the darkness
from whence the bubbles come.

To Suzie on Our Anniversary

Our daughters,
in the light of early evening,
canter across mud flat meadows.
Mermaids astride galloping seahorses,
reflecting their magic in tidal pools.

They are like their mother.
As strong-willed as the ocean's pull
and
as direct as winter winds blowing
out of the cold northeast.

They, too,
do not tolerate foolishness,
but sail a course of their very own.
And this,
this pleases me greatly.

Thank You

I have been told
that you do not get to choose your muse.
It is not an advertised position
nor can it be applied for.
It happens,
just happens.

I have also been told
that the life of one's muse,
the inspiration,
is subjected to the same unknown laws
as its acquisition.

So,
I cannot explain why you happened.
I also cannot explain why you unhappened.
Like the mystery of what the tide brings in,
it is.
Simply is.
I do, however,
wish to thank you.

Aging:
A Predatory Fish

A Predatory Fish

A thin line of red rises above the awakening Salt Pond.
I am holding tightly to my coffee.
I sit
and watch.

In the mangroves,
birds have not yet begun to stir.
Neither have my wanting wishes
which,
as always,
lie just beneath the surface.

It is a slack tide,
but there is a visceral urgency to this morning.
Drifting freely,
I wonder about you,
about me.

There were words that needed to be said,
tasks that needed to be completed.
Such needs are not softened
by the coming of the dawn,
instead, they are eroded by the salt air,
rusted by the movement of the tides.

Time,
which was once a friendly ally,
has become a predatory fish.

South Coast

The weather is angry, it is cold.
From the north Atlantic,
arctic blasts try to blow me over.
They upset me physically.
They upset me mentally.

The day is Nordic in its gray fury.
The wind eggs it on,
and the rain blows sideways.
This is not the Salt Pond with its gentle breezes.

Walking along this different shore,
which is volcanic and hostile,
I need assistance.
My balance is not what it once was.
Not good at all for self-esteem.
I am cold.
Not good for self-image.
I feel frail,
and frail is not what I want to be.
Not good at all.

Iceland

Egress

I am watching as evening descends
over the salt pond.
Physically,
I, too, am disappearing into the night,
aging.

My mind, however,
remains youthful.
Sharp as the salt air and as active
as the tidal flow.
My body, however,
like the shoreline,
is slowly eroding.

There are things my body has done
and my mind still believes are possible,
but like a pelican trying to fly into a strong wind,
we get nowhere.

It is difficult to accept such changes.
So I build seawalls of health food,
levees of exercise, and
ports for rest.

But the erosion continues,
and I progress towards my egress.

Car Keys

I am looking out at the Salt Pond
as it fades into the mist of night.
Activities have stilled,
birds have settled.
There is a quietness to the universe.

An osprey flies by at eye level,
unconcerned.
There is fog,
and it seems to be getting thicker.
A pelican lands hard in the water;
I hear the splash.
I am frightened of losing my independence.

I am lonely,
wanting one more final wow,
an electrical jolt
that takes my breath away.
I crave a new adventure,
my grip has tightened.
I am not yet ready
to surrender my car keys.

Fifty Years Later

Now with a freedom not asked for,
an independence not wanted,
I find that today I am accountable
only to my honesty.

I have thought long about such freedom
and wonder at the vast oceans of choice.
I have wondered where to travel,
what to have for dinner,
and
I have wondered
about other relationships.

I have thought long and hard about this,
weighing incoming and outgoing tides,
but after almost fifty years,
the bumps and the curves
would be in all the wrong places,
and the aroma,
the smell of another's freshly washed hair,
would be oh,
oh so very wrong.

Running to Low

This morning,
again,
I feel my age and lack of balance.
I try not to spill my coffee
as I walk out to the balcony.
Sunrise gives definition to the Salt Pond
as does the warmth of the mug to my hands.

It is no longer a slack tide;
the roots of the mangroves are exposed.
The water flows outward.
It is running to low.

I watch the agility of the diving ducks
and the steadfastness of the herons.
I watch them
with envy,
admiring their physicality.

An ibis with an injured leg
wades awkwardly,
looking for food.
I sip my cooling coffee.
I relate;
I, too, am struggling with what is.

High Stepping in the Shallows

Sitting on my balcony looking at the Salt Pond,
I wonder.
If afterlife was a fact,
not a belief,
would I choose to be here?

In addition,
I think about whether
I am afraid of dying
or
just being dead.

Thoughts like these
swim through my brain
like fish around the reef.
This is new for me.
A maiden voyage
taken gingerly
in waters I have chosen to ignore.

I look back to the Salt Pond,
thankfully distracted by a great white heron
high stepping in the shallows.

I am thinking about these things
more frequently now,
with a new appreciation
for the tide as it ebbs.

A Great White Heron

Slack Tide

Sitting on my balcony sipping coffee,
I look at the Salt Pond
and find myself thinking about
the end of my life.

That does not bother me,
not too much.
What frightens me is the slack tide.
The time between king tides and ebb tides.
I am not good at being alone.

Since you died,
there have been too many slack tides.
I have tried to fill them with work,
with swimming,
with my poetry.
But what I have missed most
is your trust
and the certainty of your touch.

A bird lands on the pond's surface,
nearly a ripple.
Will my departure be that quiet,
or will there be a loud splash?

Birthing into the Night

A hallway lit by memories,
neither the beginning nor the end
seen clearly.
The beginning facts are known
only because someone has told them to me.
The ending facts, still mostly unknown,
are hidden in the memory of what is yet
to come.

A continuing birth canal,
constructed of adobe bricks,
with an umbilical of crystal hope.
A hallway of sunlit rays
and muddy shadows that hide mistakes.

There are doors on both sides,
unnumbered,
all closed,
"Do not disturb" signs hang.

This is my journey,
not a dream nor a flashback,
not told to me by someone else.
It is an extension of my own walk.

I am finishing this story,
writing the ending.

Adding memory to memory,
adobe to adobe,
birthing into the night.

Salt Pond in Moonlight

Acknowledgments

I would like to thank my daughters, Betsy and Sarah, for their encouragement and support. In addition, I am indebted to Sean P. Callahan and Michael Hamlin, two good friends who read the poems, offered feedback, urged me to continue to write and share my work. I am also beholding to Diana Heller who initially helped organize the poems and to Susie Eyclesheimer, the lady on the couch.

All photographs taken by the author.